DON'T BE NORMAL
BE UNSTOPPABLE

Ryan Saxman

i

First edition.

Edited by Susan Strecker.
Book and cover design by Chad McComas.

Visit the author's website at www.be-unstoppable.com

To: KAELA D.

From: RyAn S.

DReAm BiG!

To our FUTURE
SuCCESS!

iii

DEDICATION

This book is dedicated to my mother, Ms. Cynthia M. Ward, for instilling the greatest values in me, never giving up on me, and seeing my true potential. She is the most amazing woman I have ever known. She raised a boy into a man as a single parent and worked countless years to provide. Even when I was doing all the wrong things in life, she never stopped loving me. For that I am forever grateful. I love you. Your son, Ryan Saxman

"You miss 100 percent of the shots you don't take."
Wayne Gretzky

TABLE OF CONTENTS

FORWARD

The intention of this book is to show readers how the way I was living was harmful to my overall health, wealth, and happiness. Television, radio, politics, Facebook, Twitter, sports, and Hollywood gossip flooded every crevice of my mind. I didn't have any long-term goals. Poor money management, fear of failure, not believing in myself, and indecision plagued my mind.

I thought that it was completely normal to watch hours of television, eat whatever I wanted, and not read. I personally needed a change. By taking action and making those needed changes, I have had more success in every aspect of my life in one year than the previous thirty. I realized that the world we create is a mirrored image of our subconscious minds, thoughts that have taken shape. It was up to me to change what I saw in the mirror. So I took charge of my life, made the difficult changes, and created a healthy lifestyle.

I will show you how making changes in my daily habits helped me achieve my goals. I wanted to be healthy and financially successful, so I changed everything about my life to create the amazing life that deep down I knew I deserved. Anything my heart desired became obtainable. The road to El Dorado lies right beneath our feet, but it is up to us to take the first step. Without true desire, repetition, and highly sought-after goals we might never become unstoppable, but with faith, focus, and unwavering determination we can truly turn any thought into reality.

1

AUTHOR'S INTRODUCTION

I was raised by my mother in a small mobile home park off Dorchester Road near Charleston, South Carolina. She was a hard-working woman making minimum wage. Together with my older sister and grandmother, we lived in a single-wide mobile home until I was nine years old.

I spent my days riding bikes with my best friend, J.B., and getting into typical little-boy mischief. No matter whether we were building forts in the woods or looking for gators in the local pond, we always made sure to get home before the street lights came on. Unfortunately around that time, my grandmother passed away at just sixty-four from heart disease. Ms. Lillian S. Ward was full of love and spoiled the heck out of me by often making my favorite foods. She was a nurse for more than twenty-five years, always caring for others. She has never left my side— she is my guardian angel and has watched over me since the day she passed. I think about her every day and can't wait to see her again.

After her passing we moved to a quaint subdivision, where I spent the next few years making new friends, getting into more mischief, and worrying about getting home before curfew. When I turned ten I would walk around the neighborhood with a broom and ask people if I could sweep their driveways. I would come back with $15 to $20. Even then, I had the entrepreneurial spirit.

When I was eleven, I started going with my mother on sales calls. She sold security systems and would go to customers' homes to give demonstrations. She paid me $10 a sale for entertaining her customers' kids. I got experience with door-knocking and, in my opinion, it takes considerable courage to knock on a stranger's front door and pitch what you're selling. My mother and I received many rejections, but she taught me that I couldn't let previous rebuffs affect her next sales pitch. I learned many valuable lessons that summer. She taught me how to be confident in the face of rejection. She instilled determination and the power of faith in me that I carry around with me to this day. That summer was my introduction to the world of sales.

We moved again when I was thirteen years old. Weary from being uprooted once again and wary of having to make new friends, I succumbed to temptation. I started smoking cigarettes and pot, drinking alcohol, stealing, and sneaking out. It was a sad but valuable time that I wouldn't change because it helped mold me into the man I am today. I learned many lessons from that period, including how not to be and the troubles that ensued because of my actions. I eventually got caught stealing and then moved up to selling marijuana at my high school. I envisioned living in a single-wide trailer for the rest of my life, on parole and having four kids by four women while I complained about my miserable life. I didn't know it then, but that was the beginning of me changing my life.

My father negatively impacted my childhood even though I only spent a few weeks with him in the summers.

The rest of the year I lived with my mother. I hated visiting him. After one particular stay with him, I returned home sobbing and told my mother how he verbally abused me, had no compassion and made me partake in detail training. That is, he felt he had to correct a deficiency. I remember one instance where my sister and I had to clean an oven with a toothbrush, making sure every inch of that stove was spotless, because we'd had an argument. Another time I had to sit at the dinner table for hours staring at cold vegetables on my plate, only allowed to leave once everyone else had gone to bed.

It seems I only remember the bad times with my father; the worst was when I was eight years old and visiting him in the Lake of the Ozarks in Missouri. He told me to carry a huge box down a staircase built into the side of a steep hill while he waited for me in the house. The stairs were wide, so I had to take a few steps in between to reach the next one down. I made it down the first few okay but misjudged one and fell down the staircase, biting through three-quarters of my tongue. I lay on the ground in immense pain, disoriented, not moving, crying, and in a pool of my own blood. Because I didn't get the box back to the house quickly, my father came out screaming at me to hurry up. He didn't even care that I was hurt. Those are the moments with him that stand out in my mind. Since then, I have had little to no communication with him.

When I was sixteen, I got a job at a local tire shop. My boss was a drunk. His wife was the sober one, but yelled more than he did. Those two were a pain to work for, but I was able to take away many valuable lessons from the job—one being that it felt awful to be unappreciated and devalued. After a few years of working at the tire shop, it was time for a change. I eventually got into residential electrical work for a few years and it really took off until the market crash in 2008. Seemingly instantly, I went from making around $800 a week to around $300. I still wanted to stay in the electrical field, so I went with the next best thing—industrial electrical work. I started out making $16.50 an hour with all the hours I wanted, but I hated that job! I worked with forty-year-olds who used drugs and had no ambition. Working at a coal power plant while breathing in coal dust and working on

420 volts was not my ideal job. I knew if I stayed there I would end up like the men I worked with. I had to get out.

Around that time my girlfriend and I found out that we were going to become parents. Months later we welcomed Tyler Saxman to the world—eight pounds and nine ounces of pure joy, the love of my life. Having a son changed me in ways that only having a child can. My mentality in life drastically changed because I just wasn't thinking about myself anymore. I wanted to make something of myself to provide an extraordinary life for my son. He is the best thing that has ever happened to me, filling my life with love and laughter. I never knew I could love someone as much as I love my son.

After four and a half years with Tyler's mother, she and I were both dissatisfied together. But, I was young and scared to leave. I told my mother about our problems and how I worried our arguing was having a negative impact on our son. She asked if I thought Tyler would be better off growing up with two unhappy parents. Our relationship had gotten to a terrible state and I knew if I stayed that was exactly what he would grow up seeing. After much turmoil, I separated from his mother.

A few months later I looked into entering the military. I didn't want to join the Marines or Army because I was against the reasons our country went to war. Not wanting to spend months at sea, I decided against the Navy. That left the Air Force and the Coast Guard. I'd have to be overseas for four years or more in the Air Force and I didn't want to be that far away from my son for that long of a period, leaving one option. The Coast Guard mainly operates within the United States and is a lifesaving organization, so I joined the Coast Guard in 2009 and never looked back. I went through boot camp up in Tracen, Cape May. Boot camp taught me two things—how to do endless hours of rifle PT and how it feels to get screamed at for two months straight. I gained an immense amount of discipline and time management skills during that training. My first unit was stationed in Yankeetown, Florida, where I stayed for the first two-and-a-half years of my career. I was federal law enforcement and a tactical boat crew member. I went on many lifesaving missions. I learned how gratifying it was to help people in situations when they needed it most. When a mother would come into the station in tears because I had saved her son and husband from a sinking boat, it was an overwhelming experience. The Coast Guard's core values are honor, respect, and devotion to duty. I practice and appreciate them on a daily basis.

Throughout my Coast Guard career I have been a part of many drug busts in South America and picked up Jamaican drug runners who were nothing more than family men and farmers doing the dirty work for the drug kingpins because they had no choice; their family's lives had been threatened. I have been a part of countless helicopter operations missions in the middle of the night to catch go-fast boats speeding across the Atlantic, desperately trying to get to the United States.

After six years, I decided to slow down and get into finance and procurement. I became a procurement specialist and got stationed in Kodiak, Alaska for two years. The terrain was brutal—it rained seven months a year and a permanent grey fog surrounded the island. I felt like I was living in a Stephen King novel. I missed sunshine and I was tired of living in places that I did not want to be. I had a job with benefits and everyone around me was always saying it could be worse, but I knew in my heart that the world had something bigger for me.

I advanced to second class petty officer, got short toured off the island, and ended up in Atlantic Beach, North Carolina—eight hours away from my now ten-year-old son. I had long since learned there was no place like home and true love and happiness resides in family—at least the ones I loved. I ended up getting an associate's degree in business administration and testing for first class petty officer.

The day I turned thirty-one I woke up at five o'clock, made a cup of coffee, grabbed a blanket from the couch, and went into my office to start writing. A year before, I'd decided I didn't want to live paycheck-to-paycheck as I'd been doing my entire adult life. There had to be a better way to live. As I sat at my desk, I wondered where and how to start. I felt unworthy. Everything I'd learned about money was negative. Many sayings that I carried around with me were: "Money is the root of all evil," "It is harder for a wealthy man to enter into the kingdom of heaven than a poor man," "Wealthy people are crooks." My belief system was enforced by an article I'd read years before about the "curse of the Power Ball winners." It stated that a high percentage of lottery winners go broke, their lives turns to ruins, and in some instances they meet a premature death.

I set out on a three-month journey to find out what I wanted to do other than live my life in the military. I dove head first into every job that I thought I would be interested in. I spoke to people in other career fields as well as owners of companies. I made sure to ask questions such as, what does the work entail? How many hours a week would I be working? What level of education and on-the-job experience is required? What does a normal day entail? What is the hourly rate? Are there areas for advancement? All these questions were answered with opportunities that did not interest me. I didn't want to work for an hourly rate. I would need to make $100 an hour and work forty hours a week to make $200,000 a year before taxes. Given my skill sets, that seemed very unrealistic.

I would need to become my own boss and set out on a journey to find out how to make the most money in the least amount of time. What skill set would put me in the place I wanted to be in? I was leaning toward sales, not manual labor. So I focused the majority of my attention toward pyramid schemed sales structure markets, residual income based sales, jewelry sales, electronic sales, and health and cosmetic sales. I tried working in these fields, but I still wasn't making the return on investment I wanted. Also, I needed to love what I would be doing. I didn't feel any passion for the jobs that I tried.

One night I went down the YouTube rabbit hole. I began watching videos about great white sharks and hours later found myself engrossed in a creative real estate investing clip. I felt something unexplainable. It was a video by Ron Legrand, "Turn $10 into $10,000 in 30 Days with Real Estate." It is a series of three videos that I watched continuously over the next few days. I didn't know it at the time, but those few days would change my life. Legrand laid out his ugly house/pretty house business and I took detailed notes and placed them in my office for the next year. Since then I have been in many mentorship programs and have learned an immense amount about real estate investing. I have found what I truly love to do. It's not a job for me, but a way of life! That is the key to a life of happiness and prosperity. Loving what you do can make all the difference.

What attracted me to real estate investing was the flexibility and freedom it could provide for me and my family. I learned how to create very profitable investment deals. I was intrigued by how much profit could be made from each deal. This allowed me to become successful while I worked as an active duty member in the United States Coast Guard.

Since getting involved in investment real estate, I have reached out to people in need—homeowners who can't make their payments or live out of state and are letting their property deteriorate. Some people are stuck paying two mortgages and need quick relief. I have helped distressed homeowners out of detrimental situations, employed contractors, real estate agents, closing companies, real estate attorneys, tax professionals, employees, and of course have constructed beautiful new homes within the community. These are true win-win scenarios that I created on a monthly basis within my business. The next best thing is the return on investment. I have created $15,000 profit margins using just $1 of my own money. I have created $30,000 profit margins using none of my own money. By understanding the fundamentals of real estate investing and amplifying my knowledge on the subject I have been able to create highly profitable deals that I can duplicate over and over again. This is the exact business model that I set out to find. Today I am a successful real estate investor and earned a six-figure income within the first year of being in business. At the time of writing this book I held over $1 million in property within my business portfolio. I created a clothing line, the real estate investing mentorship program "Motivation to Millions," and I am an author. This success is due to me changing my mindset, finding the right mentors, changing my circle of influence, and taking massive action.

Using the principles laid out in the following chapters, you can achieve the life of your dreams and become unstoppable in any endeavor you choose to go after. If I can do it, anyone can do it!

For me to achieve success I had to make significant changes in my life. The following characteristics describe me before I took action.

Procrastinator

Non-risk taker

Non-action taker

Lived for the weekends

Loved instant gratification

Blamer

Complainer

Smoker

Uncaring

Drinker

Selfish

Self-absorbed

Not a giver

Never happy, just content

Surrounded myself with narrow-minded people

Didn't take responsibility

Cared what other people thought

Feared failure

How many of these characteristics do you see in yourself? Are they common occurrences? Do they create more success or conflict in your life?

Just by asking yourself these questions you are on the right path. Write down the characteristics you wish to change and work on changing them every day. Taking action is the key to your success. Become an action taker and do not procrastinate.

For me to achieve the success that I have today I had to replace my old characteristics with new ones. I use self-affirmations, choosing a few at a time and repeating them while looking in the mirror each morning. This solidifies each characteristic for me. The following qualities are what I try to exemplify every day.

Compassion

Fearlessness

Decisiveness

Being a massive action taker

Caring

Truthfulness

Ethical

Respect

Honesty

Book reader

Goal setter

Focus

Spirituality

Giving

Thoughtfulness

Time-management conscious

CEO

Entrepreneur

Author

Loving son

Loving father

Gratefulness

How many of these characteristics do you see in yourself? It feels good to recognize these traits, doesn't it?

Being fearless completely transformed my life and is helping me reach my full potential. Once I started implementing this characteristic into my life real change started to occur. I started talking to people I wouldn't regularly talk to. I began asking questions I wouldn't regularly ask and I started to do the things that I was previously scared to do. Stepping outside of my comfort zone allowed me to live for the first time in my life! I realized fear was holding me back from achieving greatness. It was a wall built up in my mind that paralyzed me for years, but I pushed it aside and started living by these words:

Once you become fearless, your life becomes limitless!

Changing my life started with a single thought—there has to be a better way. I just needed to start thinking about the positive characteristics I wanted to embody. Just doing so started drastically changing my world for the better. I didn't know it at the time, but I had become a creator and not just an observer. I strongly believe that the creators in this world get rewarded tenfold more than the average person. What I mean by becoming a creator is making your thoughts into reality—for example, take a look at Oprah Winfrey, Bill Gates, Thomas Edison, and Elon Musk. All blazed new paths, making their thoughts into reality and not accepting anything less. Their successes are known around the world! We all have what it takes to achieve the same levels of success.

Compassion is another characteristic that has played a pivotal role in my success. I picked up reading around the time I knew I needed to make a change. Within the first year I had listened to over thirty books, my favorite being *The Divine Matrix* by Gregg Braden. The author discusses how simply observing matter seems to change it. He journeyed to the hills of Tibet, where he spoke with a monk in a small temple where he had lived the entirety of his life. Mr. Braden asked the monk what was the secret to the universe. The monk replied, "Compassion." Such a simple yet powerful answer. I carry this with me. Deciding to fill my life with compassion was the moment I started seeing massive results in achieving the goals I had set for myself.

2

NORMAL

According to the Merriam Webster dictionary, normal is defined as "conforming to a type, standard, or regular pattern." (Also known as conformity.) Definitions of normal vary by person, time, place, and situation. It changes along with societal standards and norms. The most common behaviors in society equal the majority of behaviors in a defined area.

A friend of mine is a marriage and family therapist. She shared something with me that she learned in graduate school. She always says that normal isn't normal. Normal is what we know. That is, whatever is familiar to us seems like the norm. In my mind I was normal.

The following is a snapshot of what my life looked like before I took massive action to improve it. On an average work day my alarm went off at 6:30 a.m. I'd hit snooze twice and check my smartphone for texts, social media, local news, and emails before finally dragging myself out of bed. After showering and dressing, I'd scarf down a bowl of cereal. Then I'd hop in my new convertible Camaro, turn on the latest tunes, and head off to work at the Coast Guard. The majority of my thoughts were focused on social media and LeBron James. Throughout my day I discussed political events, news, and entertainment with coworkers. When lunch rolled around I would head out with a few coworkers, usually to get fast food and spend my time surfing the web looking for other job opportunities. I wasn't happy with my current position in life. I was only content.

I received my college education using the GI bill, so luckily I wasn't paying back huge college loans. A few of my coworkers received their degrees before they entered the service. They had huge student loans that were hurting their current financial situations. We'd head back to work and complete our daily tasks while we laughed, joked, and watched ridiculous short videos.

A few days a week I would pick up a six pack of beer on my way home and wait for my friends to come over to watch basketball, drink, and play video games. Besides working out a few days a week, playing softball, and eating out with friends occasionally, most of my time was spent in front of the TV, tablet, or computer. I felt that I deserved to relax when I wasn't working. Of course, I traveled, spent time with family, and went on a few vacations each year. I thought my life was average. I never really thought about changing. It took years of me being just content and tired of my bosses to even think about making a change. I was essentially just going through the motions of life. I wanted to start thriving, not just surviving.

The following are ten events in which I engaged every day.

1. Hitting the snooze button each morning.
   According to a study by the French tech firm

Withings, an extended stay in bed actually makes a person more tired and can lead to lack of concentration and wellbeing throughout the day. I find myself most alert when I immediately wake up. Not hitting the snooze button and falling back to sleep helps with overall mood, productivity throughout the day, and a sense of enjoyment.

Key Point: By hitting the snooze button and waking up tired every day, I unknowingly set myself up for failure.

2. Checking my smart phone before getting out of bed. By doing so, I filled my mind with non-essential information, including news of incidents in my local community, the latest trends in Hollywood, and sports highlights. That non-essential information stayed with me for the next several hours as I surfed YouTube and Facebook looking at my friends' pictures, posting selfies, and commenting on random

posts. According to a study in the Harvard Business Review, prolonged Facebook usage significantly reduces physical health, mental health, and life satisfaction because comparing one's life to others' results in discontentment. Prolonged exposure to social media and the lack of real world interaction can produce less meaningful real-life experiences. I was unaware that what I was doing could be harmful to my overall health and wellbeing.

Key Point: The information that I was choosing to put in my mind was not at all beneficial to creating any kind of success in my life.

3. Breakfast. I loved to eat Cocoa Puffs, French Toast Crunch, and for more of a healthy choice, Honey Bunches of Oats. I liked eating cereal in the morning because it was quick and easy. Little did I know I was setting myself up to consume more carbs in one sitting than my body needed in

an entire day. According to information provided by Massive Health's Eatery iPhone app, breakfast really is the most important meal of the day. The study shows that people who eat breakfasts high in sugar consume more food throughout the day. Eating a healthy breakfast may prevent low blood sugar levels in between meals and thus improve self-regulation in eating throughout the day. People who eat a balanced breakfast tend to have healthier diets throughout the day. People who eat breakfast high in sugar eat 7 percent more food throughout the day and choose unhealthier options. According to Healthline, most breakfast cereals fall short of their claims of being healthy. They are loaded with sugars and refined carbs. After eating cereal in the morning, blood sugar levels will eventually crash and the body will then crave another high-carb meal, creating a cycle of overeating and choosing unhealthy options throughout the day.

Key Point: Eating an unbalanced breakfast caused my body to crave higher-carb meals throughout the day, ultimately leading to weight gain and an unhealthy lifestyle.

4. Driving my beautiful new convertible Camaro. I bought that car because I liked it and wanted to keep up with everyone else, even though I couldn't afford a $28,000 car. My monthly payments were around $360. My insurance was about $110 a month. That was $470 that could have been better spent elsewhere. I was making around $40,000 dollars a year and had just bought a huge liability. To comfortably afford a $28,000 vehicle, I would need to make around $115,000 per year.

Key Point: By spending money that I did not have to keep up with the status quo, I decreased my credit score and decreased my monthly income. Both are very important aspects of achieving success.

5. Getting my associate's degree. A few of my coworkers had insurmountable student loans that would take years to pay back. I was lucky enough to join the military and use tuition assistance to receive my associate's degree. My coworkers, on the other hand, had received their degrees before joining the military. I spoke with one about his student debt. His associate's degree cost him around $7,000. Once he had completed that, he transferred to a more prestigious four-year college to complete his bachelor's degree. He ended up spending around $40,000 for tuition and board, totaling $47,000 on his education. According to Forbes Magazine, student loan debt is at an all-time high. Over 44 million borrowers have a total debt of $1.3 trillion in America alone. The average student loan debt is around $37,000, with only 27 percent of college graduates working in the career field they chose. I believe that the value of a degree has dropped

in the last three decades. This played a huge role when it came to me looking for a new career.

Key point: I decided I wanted to become the CEO of my own company. I wanted to achieve $1 million a year in profits, but with continuing and using my college degree I personally did not see that being achievable.

6. Buying fast food. Before I decided to make a change in my life I pretty much ate whatever I wanted. I wasn't a couch potato by any means, so I was able to keep the weight off—but every day after lunch I was exhausted and I didn't know why. I found out that it was from overeating and consuming too much processed food. According to a study by healthline.com, eating too much fast food can lead to health issues such as depression, high blood pressure, headaches, acne, heart disease, weight gain, and Type 2 diabetes. I never really looked at any studies that showed the side effects of eating too much fast food. Like

many other things, moderation is the key to consuming fast food.

Key point: I will be the first to admit that I love fast food, but for longevity and a healthy lifestyle, fast food should be eaten sparingly.

7. Consuming information about current events, politics, and entertainment. I used to spend about three hours a day watching television, an hour playing video games, and an hour or two on social media. I loved watching basketball games and enjoyed watching a few movies throughout the week. Most of my conversations revolved around what I was putting in my head. In retrospect, I wasn't enjoying reality throughout the week. I never thought once about picking up a book. Back then I thought that wasn't nearly as entertaining as watching LeBron's dunk highlights.

Dr. Graham Davey completed a study on how media violence affects one's state of mind. His study shows that violent media exposure can contribute to depression, anxiety, stress, and even post-traumatic stress disorder. In addition to watching violent movies during the week, I woke up every morning and turned on the news that flooded my mind with murders, abductions, and serious car accidents. I didn't understand that it was negatively affecting my mindset.

According to a publication from Harvard Medical School, music plays a vital role in relieving stress for surgeons in the operating room and for patients with their recovery. Music plays an increasing role in all aspects of healing and overall wellbeing. It has also been linked to treating psychiatric disorders, improving creativity, and helping to power through a work out. With such a powerful influence on the human mind I became aware of what I was watching and listening to. I stopped allowing so many negative TV shows, movies, and songs in my life. I became more aware of what I was allowing myself to watch and listen to.

Key Point: By allowing so many outside influences to consume my thoughts, it left no room for my own creativity.

8. Playing video games. It wasn't enough that I loved violent movies. I also loved to play violent video games. My two favorite video games were *Tom Clancy's Ghost Recon: Wildland* and *Grand Theft Auto V*. Both games are about blood, gore, and violence. At the time I didn't see anything wrong with playing those types of games. Today I still do enjoy the occasional video game but mostly spend my time doing more productive things. According to ProCon.org, more than 90 percent of pediatricians in the United States say prolonged exposure to violent media can heighten childhood aggression. This can desensitize us, heightening aggression and increasing acts of violence toward others.

Key point: If we are what we choose to put in our minds, shouldn't we be more conscious of what we watch and listen to?

9. The Coast Guard. It treated me well—I saw and did things that I would not have otherwise been able to. I had accomplished that milestone in my life and was ready to move on. There was something greater out there for me. I just had to take the correct action to achieve what I wanted to. According to a survey conducted by VisualCV, 60 percent of Americans hope to change jobs. Being in a job that I didn't want to be in directly affected the outcome of my day-to-day life. It affected my productivity, creativity, overall happiness, and drive. I was disengaged from my daily activities within my job. I was surrounded by people that I didn't want to be around and I ended up doing the bare minimum to get by.

I didn't realize it, but if I truly wanted to be happy in life I needed to love what I did to make a living. I couldn't be unhappy at work, then flip a switch and expect everything to be great when I left.

Key Point: Being unhappy with my current job affected all aspects of my life in some way or another.

10. Drinking alcohol. I used alcohol to relax and unwind from the day. I justified it by saying I'd had a hard day at work and deserved a drink. According to drugfreeworld.org, alcohol is best understood as a drug that reduces a person's ability to think rationally and distorts his or her judgment. Classified as a depressant, the amount of alcohol consumed determines the type of effect that it has on a person. I would regularly have three to four drinks several times a week. I made poorer decisions, ate unhealthily, and got tired earlier in the evening. When I did start

drinking I was unproductive for the rest of the night.

Key Point: I understood that alcohol consumption could have a negative impact on my ability to achieve high levels of success.

"If you want to soar like an eagle in life, you can't be flocking with the turkeys." Warren Buffett—investor, philanthropist, self-made billionaire

In my mind I was average. If I wanted to continue down that path I think that it would have been perfectly okay. I paid my bills, I was a tax-paying citizen, I cared for people, and I volunteered my time to help others through the Coast Guard but, since I wanted to achieve more in life, I would have to make a change. I could not continue the way I was living and expect to have the freedom to travel the world, purchase my dream home, and provide my son with possibilities early on in life that he might not otherwise have had. This is my journey.

3

YOUR WHY

I quickly understood that I would need a powerful reason to change. I spent a few days coming up with very powerful and meaningful whys. When times got tough, when new problems arose, when I found myself out of my comfort zone, my why helped me not give up. I learned that becoming successful would have to become a way of life, not just a one-night sensation. I knew I would need to work hard on a daily basis. When coming up with my whys, if I did not feel any emotion, I knew I needed a deeper why.

It is important to have more than one why. I have put my whys in this book for three reasons: First, so that you may get a firsthand look into my life and what pushes me forward. Second, so you can get a better understanding of who I am. Third, they could provide you with a good starting point.

My Whys

I want to spend more time with my family.

I want to surround myself with successful people.

I want financial freedom.

I want to travel the world.

I want to give my son the keys to success and a better life than I had.

I want to repay my mother for never giving up on me.

Your why gives you the motivation to keep pushing forward. The more motivation you have, the quicker you can reach your goal. There are three situations that have provided me with motivation to better my circumstances in life. Each one of these instances has shown me why I should appreciate life. The first would have to be having my son. My actions directly affect my son's life, so everything I do has to benefit him. I wanted to provide

Tyler with resources early on so that he can achieve whatever interests him. My productivity grew, and my mental focus and faith became stronger. My decision making became more methodical and time management skills increased. That was when I decided to join the military in order to provide great health care and pay for four years of college for him. I felt unconditional love, happiness, purpose, motivation, persistence, and gratitude. I use this to fuel my why.

The second situation that I use to reflect on is a loved one passing. One thing that gets put into perspective for me is the short amount of time that I have here on earth. I see just how precious time really is; it can end at any moment. I realized I was wasting a large amount of my time by living the way I was. Reflecting on this situation, I try to make the most out of every day. Each day I try to be productive, kind, and try to give back in some way. I realized the importance of friends and family and understand that I should not take them for granted. I try not to put too much want in material possessions, yet I do like really nice things. I do understand their place and purpose and try not to become materialistic. I gained a sense of gratitude for simply being alive and benefited spiritually. My relationship with God becomes stronger and I understand that there is a life after this one. I choose not just to live for this life but also the next.

Key question: What gets placed in perspective for you by a loved one passing?

The third situation in my life that I gain motivation from is having strong relationships with friends and family. When I am surrounded with friends and family my happiness and confidence are at their highest. Having good relationships within my life sparks creativity, excitement, and passion. According to a study completed by the Harvard Medical School, " ... a relative lack of social ties is associated with depression and later-life cognitive decline, as well as with increased mortality. One study, which examined data from more than 309,000 people, found that lack of strong relationships increased the risk of premature death from all causes by 50 percent—an effect on mortality risk roughly comparable to smoking up to fifteen cigarettes a day, and greater than obesity and physical inactivity." Having a healthy social life provides me with a positive outlook on life and motivates me to keep moving forward. It also helps me be less stressed.

Each one of the three situations that I use to empower my why could help you as well. It can give you a starting point to create a very powerful why in your own life. When I bring creativity, compassion, excitement, confidence, and happiness into any new project I am setting myself up for success.

These three experiences that I use in a positive light are based in birth, death, and love. They put into perspective what I truly value in life. With every new venture I embark upon I keep these lessons in the front of my mind.

"The two most important days of your life are the day you were born and the day you find out why." Mark Twain—author of the *Adventures of Huckleberry Finn* and regarded by some as the father of American literature

REBOOT AND REPROGRAM

This is one of the most important chapters for me.

The quicker I changed my thoughts and actions the quicker I started seeing my ideas become reality. Being lazy, comfortable, and average was not going to get me the success that I was striving for. Looking back at when I made a serious change my life, it ended up being thanks to one simple thought. "I want to live life on my own terms." That thought was when I made a serious decision to change my ways of life for the better. I didn't just want to achieve success, I wanted to become unstoppable! Without taking action no change would have occurred.

First, I needed to reboot. According to the Merriam-Webster dictionary, reboot is "to shut down and restart." I needed to produce a distinctly new version of myself and make a change to establish a new beginning. This task seemed very challenging since I had lived an average life for so many years. I started doing research into habits and how many days it took to stop a habit. I read a book called *Psycho-Cybernetics* by Maxwell Maltz, in which he suggests it takes about twenty-one days to form a new habit. I wanted to approach the rebooting phase with this in mind.

I had felt like I was floating in an ocean without any direction, waiting for the currents to pull my life in any direction it deemed fit. I needed to build a vessel, decide on a destination, and sail straight to it. I knew I was going to need to build a strong ship. In my mind, if I built a small sail boat, I would capsize. On the other hand, if I built a seaworthy ship I would greatly increase my chances reaching my destination.

I needed to commit just a few minutes a day for the next twenty-one days to meditate. The first week consisted of five minutes a day; the second week, I increased my meditation time to seven minutes a day, and for the third and final week I meditated ten minutes a day. I did all my meditating first thing in the morning. This allowed my mind to be very clear and also prevented me from coming up with an excuse later in the day not to do it. I believe that success is all about commitment and this was a great first lesson in following through with what I said I would do. This was my first test.

I downloaded a meditation app on my smartphone. I could choose from calming ambient noises to streams or thunderstorms. I liked to mix it up a bit from day to day. A few times I even went over the time limit I set for myself. I soon bought a spiral notebook and wrote in it every morning, listing my goals. I placed it next to my bed for easy access. Dr. Gail Matthews, a psychology professor at the Dominican University in California, completed an interesting study on the science of goal setting. She gathered over 150 people from all walks of life. She categorized those individuals into two groups: those who wrote down their goals and those who did not. Her conclusion was that those who wrote down their goals on a regular basis achieved their goals on a much higher level than those participants who did not. Her study goes on to show that you're even more likely to achieve your goals and dreams if you share them with a friend or family member who believes in you.

My first week of meditation consisted of thinking about absolutely nothing. I realized that I never gave my brain a break. A study completed at the University of Maryland School of Medicine showed that the average person has anywhere between 12,000 to 60,000 thoughts per day. It concluded that 80 percent of those thoughts were negative and 95 percent of thoughts were repetitive. The study showed that the quality of our internal communication directly affects our external bodies. A French philosopher named Pierre Teilhard de Chardin said, "We are not human beings having a spiritual experience. We are spiritual beings having a human experience." I believe that our feelings and thoughts can create stress, depression, happiness, and gratitude. All can be draining to the human mind and body. This is why I wanted to work on clearing out my mind, body, and soul. I wanted to work on my inner self first to change my life around me. I started by focusing on my breathing. I wanted to clear my mind and become grateful for each and every breath. I tend to overcomplicate my life, so I wanted to simplify this experience as much as possible. My goal was to become overwhelmed with a sense of gratitude and happiness for just being able to breathe, no thoughts of anything else. I started to understand the power of meditation within the first day. It was an amazing introduction to stepping outside my comfort zone and trying something new. I wanted to use the first week as a building block and enter into weeks two and three with a great appreciation for what I was doing for my mind, body, and soul.

After I spent seven days meditating, I gained a tremendous amount of appreciation for just being alive. The opportunity to turn my dreams into reality gave me much happiness. Before meditating that thought never crossed my mind.

I wanted to spend week two focusing on one why a day for seven minutes and understanding what my reasons were for changing my life and creating massive success. I had never held a single thought for seven minutes straight. I had no idea of the outcome before I went into week two of meditation. I was stepping outside my comfort zone once again. Nevertheless, I was excited to embark on my transformation from living average. I knew my whys would propel me to keep chasing my dreams and moving forward when I wanted to quit.

I felt a sense of emotion come over me when I focused on my whys. A major benefit of thinking about one thought for seven minutes and feeling the emotion from that thought is that it stays with me. I think back to not just the thought but also the feeling I felt and my why became amplified. I hold my whys close to my heart and I recommend that you do the same.

The second week of meditation was very powerful for me. It put in perspective what was truly important to me and solidified why I was making a change in my life. I felt a strong sense of purpose after that week. It was important for me to spend time meditating on my whys because it is my belief that they will help carry me to my ideal life. In every action that I take my whys are always with me.

During the third and final week of meditation I wanted to focus on positive affirmations. The goal that I wanted to achieve was to gain feelings of fearlessness, tenacity, strength, and fortitude, which would help me become unstoppable in any endeavor that I chose to accomplish. Positive affirmations have been used by some of the most successful and intelligent people the world has ever known: Albert Einstein, Oprah Winfrey, Elon Musk, Napoleon Hill, and Tony Robbins. I believe that visualizations and positive affirmations go hand-in-hand. I not only said that I was confident, but I mentally visualized it as well. I pictured myself in a crowded room, confidently introducing myself to some of the top businesses. Some well-known actors that have used self-visualization successfully include Denzel Washington, Jim Carrey, and Will Smith. A few others in the business world include Bill Gates, Warren Buffett, and Grant Cardone. They all use the power of visualizations along with positive affirmations to catapult their lives into a different stratosphere.

"I think it is possible for ordinary people to choose to be extraordinary." Elon Musk—CEO of Tesla, Founder of SpaceX, and self-made billionaire

Here are the seven affirmations I used:

1. My body is healthy, my mind is brilliant, my soul is tranquil.
2. I acknowledge my self-worth; my confidence is soaring.
3. I am a powerhouse; I am indestructible.
4. I possess the qualities to be extremely successful.
5. I am the creator of my own destiny.
6. I will radiate love and compassion into the world.
7. I will achieve more than I ever thought possible.

While meditating on each positive affirmation daily, I gained a sense of accomplishment. I started to understand that my thoughts directly correlated with my reality. If I thought I was a champion, then I became a champion. I became emotionally attached to each positive affirmation and visualized each one as if it was my reality. This week was profound for me and put in perspective just how powerful our minds really are. By aligning my thoughts and energy with the exact thing I wanted to become, I created a new reality for myself. I was working on creating the law of attraction within my life.

This carried on this meditation period for more than twenty-one days. I thought if I wanted to become truly unstoppable I should use this meditation technique at least on a weekly basis. I understand that some of the most intelligent and successful people never stop learning or trying to become better. This meditation period was meant to be an astonishing jump start to my new self.

Once I completed the rebooting phase I entered into the reprogramming phase. This phase allowed me to place new positive thoughts in my mind about how I perceived myself. This led to massive confidence within myself, which then led to me gaining knowledge on the correct actions I needed to take in order to achieve massive success.

MASSIVE CONFIDENCE + CORRECT MASSIVE ACTION =
GREAT ACHIEVEMENT

In reprogramming my mind I first conditioned my subconscious mind to visualize my success. I had never tried self-visualization and affirmation techniques before. The very first book that I read once I knew I needed to make a change was *The Magic of Believing* by Claude M. Bristol. Within the pages of that book he discusses the power of the subconscious mind. He states that the power of the subconscious mind is endless. I wanted to find out for myself what kind of effect would this have in my life. It is my belief that the subconscious mind is essentially the energy within us that connects everything in space and time. It was my goal to start looking at life as an energy source, finding a deeper meaning and bringing great depth into the world around me. I wanted to start attracting what it was that I wanted in my life. By focusing on what type of energy I was emitting to the world, I was able to attract what was needed in my life to create massive success. I reprogrammed my mind to tap the powers of the mind, in order to perceive the world in ways I have never done so before.

I had many different visions of success for myself, but I tried visualizing my ideal life. In doing so, I visualized me having a very successful real estate investing company and plenty of free time to travel and help people around the world. I had an amazing wife who was funny, charismatic, intelligent, outgoing, and beautiful inside and out. I was able to spend time with my family on a more frequent basis. I had friends whom I not only loved to be around but looked up to and gained inspiration from. I gave back tremendous amounts of time and money to kids who were in less than fortunate situations. This was the start of me reprogramming my subconscious mind with visions that were very specific, focused, and clear. For my subconscious mind to take the correct actions it must know exactly what I want out of life.

"El Dorado, a country rich beyond all precedent in gold and jewels, lies at every man's door. Your bonanza lies under your feet." Claude M. Bristol

I used Tony Robbins's priming method to help reprogram my mind. Robbins empowers millions of people around the world and is the number one life and business strategist in the United States. His methods, in my opinion, are some of the best in the world for creating a new you. I have seen his work and it is truly inspiring to see what people can achieve with unrelenting faith, focus, and drive.

PRIMING METHOD

1. I sat down with my eyes closed and raised my hands over my head.
2. I started breathing heavily in and out through my nose for three sets of thirty breaths.
3. On each exhale, I pulled my arms down each time making fists.

4. After completing three sets, my mind was then in an altered state, allowing me to replace any negative thoughts that I might have had with feelings of self-love and confidence.

I used this method to replace any limiting beliefs I had about myself. It was very easy, once in this state of mind, to reprogram my thought process. I use the priming method frequently to make sure my thoughts are positive. I believe self-love and confidence are the two feelings most lacking in our society. Once I reprogrammed my mind with overwhelming feelings of self-love and confidence, my happiness increased.

I hope you find great success if you use these strategies. When life and circumstances change I go back and go through the rebooting and reprogramming phase. This allows me to visualize my new ideal life, new goals, and thoughts that I want to express outward into the world.

"Whatever we plant in our subconscious mind and nourish with repetition and emotion will one day become reality."
Earl Nightingale—author and American radio speaker

5

BELIEF AND FOCUS

I believe many successful people believe in themselves. I knew I needed unfaltering focus to prevent my dreams from being just that—dreams. I had to reboot my belief system and reprogram myself so I *could* believe in myself. That is why this chapter follows the rebooting and reprogramming phase. Without the belief in myself and intense focus needed to become unstoppable my dreams would never be attainable. This chapter outlines a few people in history who have reached their dreams and impacted history despite insurmountable odds.

So many great people have become successful, in part, due to their mentors, someone they could look up to or confide in. I found people in history who I admire and who have done extraordinary things within their lives. I wrote short biographies about their lives. I study them and keep them close in my mind. This allows their struggles, achievements, and what they were able to overcome to inspire me on a daily basis.

It is my honor to start with a man who is near and dear to my heart, Jesus Christ. Jesus was born in Bethlehem around 6 B.C. in a stable. Not much is known of his younger years, but his life and ministry have touched millions of people's lives around the world for thousands of years. Jesus was very poor growing up but had a very loving mother named Mary. Jesus worked as a carpenter until he was thirty years old. Around that age he was baptized by John the Baptist and set out on a forty-day fast through the Judean desert. He was tempted by the devil on three occasions: the devil tempted Jesus by offering to turn stone into bread, then the devil offered to cast himself off the top of a mountain where an angel would save him, and lastly the devil offered Jesus all the kingdoms in the world. Jesus refused temptation all three times and completed his fast. Upon returning to Galilee, Jesus picked up twelve disciples while preaching the gospel. Early in his ministry while at a wedding, Jesus turned water into wine. This was the first documented event of Jesus's glory. He went on healing the sick, correcting disabilities, and providing hearing and vision where there had been none, all the while preaching the word of God. Throughout his travels, Jesus developed a large following. Upon entering Jerusalem, while riding a donkey, Jesus was greeted by a large number of people with palm branches praising him as the son of David and the son of God.

The Pharisees heard of a man proclaimed by his followers as the Messiah. They felt highly threatened and portrayed Jesus's teachings as being evil. They feared the love and admiration Jesus was receiving and felt he had to be stopped. They set out to arrest Jesus, but before they could it was documented that Jesus and his twelve disciples had one last dinner, known as the Last Supper. Jesus foretold one of his disciples, Peter, that he would deny knowing Jesus three times before the rooster crowed that day. Jesus also said "I have eagerly desired to eat this Passover with you before I suffer. For I tell you, I will not eat it again until it finds fulfillment in the kingdom of

God." At the end of the Last Supper Jesus instituted the Eucharist, which signified the covenant between God and humans.

Early the next morning, temple guards of the Sanhedrin arrested Jesus. He was taken to the high court and held on charges of proclaiming he was the king of the Jews. He was ultimately sentenced to death. He was beaten, mocked, spit on, and laughed at. A crown of thorns was placed upon his head, a cross on his back, and nails driven through his hands and feet. All this happened within twelve hours of arrest. Jesus's last words on the cross were, "It is finished." Translated from Greek, tetelastai means "to finish, or to fulfill". A book was written by more than forty contributors, taking almost 1,500 years to write between the years 1400 B.C. to 90 A.D. The book has the word of God. It is historically accurate and does not contradict itself one time. The book is flawless—God wanted many different viewpoints throughout history for us to see his plan for humanity. This book is titled The Bible and has gone to sell more than 3.9 billion copies around the world and is the number-one bestselling book in existence.

Jesus chose to die for our sins on the cross for us to receive everlasting life in the kingdom of heaven. For this Jesus gave the ultimate sacrifice for all of mankind, in my eyes and the eyes of billions throughout history he is the greatest man to ever set foot on this planet. Jesus had the ability to do this by utilizing two values, belief and focus. For this, I personally want to say thank you

John 3:16 For God so loved the world, that he gave his only begotten son, that whosoever believeth in him should not perish, but have everlasting life.

Nelson Mandela, birth name "Rolihlahla" meaning "troublemaker," was born on July 18, 1918 in Mvezo, a small village in South Africa located near the Mbhashe River. The village consisted of around 400 villagers, mud huts with straw roofs, sheep, donkeys, and plenty of farmland. He spent most of his childhood herding goats and playing with his thirteen brothers and sisters. With both his parents being illiterate it would have been very easy for Mandela to grow up without any education. Luckily his parents understood the value of education and sent him to a Methodist school at the age of seven. Two years into schooling he received his first name by his teacher—she called him "Nelson." Mandela went on to attend a mission school, learning English, native history, and geography. He soon progressed and started school at Fort Hare University. Mandela had dreams of becoming a lawyer. His education through the next few years was plagued by dropping out, getting arrested for being involved with protests, and his father threatening to force an arranged marriage if he did not go back to school. Mandela ran off to Johannesburg, where he worked as a mine security officer and met a gentleman who got him back into a law firm. Mandela then went back to Fort Hare University, graduating in 1943.

Mandela married Evelyn Mase in 1944 and together they had two sons. The first died in infancy. They had a rocky marriage, and losing their son exacerbated their problems. Around that time Mandela began the University of the Witwatersrand. He was in and out of that college for the next nine years and left in 1952 without a degree. After leaving college, Mandela participated in a civil disobedience campaign against six unjust laws. Mandela and nineteen others were charged criminally and sentenced to nine months in prison. That year Mandela created the first black law firm in South Africa, Mandela and Tumbo. Mandela and his wife stayed together for more than ten years but separated in 1958. After their divorce, Mandela stepped up his efforts to regain freedom and democracy within the country.

In 1960, police killed about seventy unarmed protestors in Sharpeville, South Africa. This led to the country's first state of emergency, where thousands of countrymen and women were put on trial. Everyone was eventually acquitted of the charges. Mandela took it upon himself to write to the Prime Minister, requesting a non-racial constitution. If the constitution wasn't rewritten then a national strike would be placed against the country, consisting of a series of explosions. These events took place on December 16, 1961. In January of 1962, Mandela left South Africa to gain support in the armed struggle against tyranny, genocide, and poverty within his country. Upon re-entering South Africa, Mandela was picked up at a road block and detained. He was charged with leaving the country without a permit and trying to gain support against the established government. He was sentenced to five years in prison. In 1963, the government raided a secret hideout used by communist party activists and evidence was found involving sabotage. Evidence from the raid directly linked Mandela to these criminal offenses and he was put on trial once again.

Mandela was now facing the death penalty for trying to overthrow the state, but while on trial his speech became immortalized in the struggle for freedom against the tight grip of tyranny. Nelson Mandela spoke about wanting a democratic and free society. His wish was for every man, woman, and child to live in harmony and be afforded equal opportunity. This idea Mandela lived to achieve and he was prepared to die for if he must.

The next day, Mandela and seven others were sentenced to life in prison. Mandela spent the next twenty-seven years in prison. Within those years Mandela rejected more than three conditional offers of release. He once was quoted as saying, "I went for a long holiday for twenty-seven years." Mandela became a free man on August 12, 1988. He was finally released from prison because of inside and outside political pressure for the government to end segregation and discrimination on the grounds of race. One year later Mandela graduated with an LLB from the University of South Africa. In 1991 Mandela was elected African National Congress President and replaced his longtime friend, Oliver Tambo. A few years later in 1993 Mandela and his friend FW de Klerk jointly won the Nobel Peace Prize for the peaceful end to a radical regime, as well as for laying the foundation for a new democracy in South Africa.

A year later in 1994, at the age of seventy-six, Mandela legally voted for the first time. That same year he became the first democratic president in South African history. President Mandela stayed true to his word and resigned his presidency after a five-year term and a successful presidency. Mandela continued his efforts by creating the Nelson Mandela foundation and gave back to the people of South Africa. He also supported over twenty-five different charities throughout his life. He traveled the world, bringing in millions of dollars to help his people. He also spread awareness of the harsh injustices that his people faced every day.

After years of fighting oppression and nearly giving his life multiple times for his beliefs, spending decades in prison and never losing sight of his purpose, Nelson Mandela changed a nation. In 2013, Nelson Mandela was laid to rest in his home in Johannesburg, South Africa. He died at ninety-five, and what a life he lived. With unwavering belief and focus, Nelson Mandela not only changed a tyrannical government but also the face of a nation, one of the most dangerous governments on the planet at the time. He also landed in the hearts of millions of people around the world. He spread his message of love, democracy, and freedom and won a Noble Peace Prize. One man, one belief, and one focus will change the world. Do you see the power?

Mother Teresa, birth name Agnes Bojaxhiu, was born in 1910 in Skopje, Macedonia. She was baptized the day after her birth. Her father was an entrepreneur who died mysteriously when Agnes was just eight years old. Some say he was poisoned due to his political position within the town. Her mother took good care of her for the remainder of her childhood, instilling in her compassion and a strong commitment toward helping others. Agnes's mother used to say, "My child, never eat a single mouthful unless you are sharing it with others." These deeply rooted values would follow Agnes throughout her life.

Agnes was in school throughout her childhood and sang solos in the local Sacred Heart choir. At the age of twelve, Agnes felt the calling from God to lead a very religious life. She followed that path and when she turned eighteen, she joined the Sisters of Loreto in Dublin and took the name Sister Mary Teresa. In 1931, Sister Mary Teresa traveled to India to begin her career as a teacher in the slums of Calcutta. Sister Mary Teresa became fluent in both Bengali and Hindi. She taught history and geography to her students. Her goal was simple—to alleviate poverty through education.

In 1937, Sister Mary Teresa vowed her life to one of obedience, chastity, and poverty. Upon her final vow it was custom among the Loreto nuns to take on the title of Mother. Now known as "Mother Teresa," she continued teaching at Saint Mary's and became school principal in 1944. Mother Teresa's time teaching was not easy; she lived on little to no money in one of the poorest slums in the region. Additionally, the region was plagued by two of the harshest famines in history.

Mother Teresa left the school in 1946 for a new calling. She stated that Christ spoke to her and wanted her to work in the slums in Calcutta, aiding the sickest and poorest people. Mother Teresa spent the next twenty years healing the sick and educating the poor. Donations enabled her to open multiple health clinics, including one to help lepers, and an orphanage. She was recognized by Pope Paul VI and awarded the Decree of Praise for her decades of humanitarian efforts. During that time she also received the honor of being named the Jewel of India—the most prestigious award given out by the country to any civilian. Mother Teresa also won the Nobel Peace Prize for bringing help for our suffering humanity. The award came with a cash prize of $190,000, which she donated to build more homes for the poor.

Mother Teresa died in 1997 at the age of eighty-seven. At that time more than 4,000 missionaries of charities had given their lives to helping her cause and over 600 foundations had been created in more than 120 countries. In 2003 she was canonized by Pope St. Francis as Saint Teresa of Calcutta. Her legacy will live on, grow, and be glorified throughout history.

Saint Teresa of Calcutta devoted her life to helping millions of most impoverished people. She emulated selflessness and compassion in all of her efforts. Her charitable work was astonishing and love for the poor overpowering. She created her masterpiece—one that will be remembered throughout time—with belief and focus.

"Spread love everywhere you go. Let no one ever come to you without leaving happier." Mother Teresa

A few other honorable mentions include Dr. Naveen Jain, Grant Cardone, and Ellen DeGeneres. These three people emulate belief and focus in themselves in order to achieve great success as well as give back to people in need. I use them, among others, to keep me motivated.

Dr. Naveen Jain was born in 1959 to a very impoverished family in New Delhi, India. When he was twenty years old he completed his engineering degree at the Indian Institute of Technology Roorkee. Soon after, he moved to America to chase his dreams. He looked up to billionaires and strived to become one. His first job was with a company named Unisys, located in New Jersey, as part of a business-exchange program. He soon moved to Silicon Valley, where he worked for multiple startup companies and in 1989 joined Microsoft, flourishing within the company. In 1996 Dr. Naveen Jain co-founded a company named Info Space, which made and lost hundreds of millions of dollars due to the dot com crash in the early 2000s.

Dr. Naveen Jain then co-founded a company named Intelius and quickly grew its revenue stream into the millions. He also founded companies such as TalentWise, Moon Express, Bluedot, and Viome. In 2018 I saw him speak at Grant Cardone's 10x Growth Con at the Mandalay Bay in Las Vegas. There he spoke about flying to the moon and mining platinum for fusion reactors here on Earth to solve the world's energy problems. Those reactors haven't even been created yet. Also, he founded Viome, a company that detects nutrients and toxins to help solve the world's health issues and that could cure diseases altogether. He is using his money to give back to this world in ways that are ahead of his time. He is a true visionary of the twenty-first century and is creating an amazing legacy. He is a wonderful example of what belief and focus can do in one's life.

Grant Cardone was born in 1958 in Lake Charles, Louisiana. He was the fourth of five children and grew up in a loving family. His father passed away at a young age, leaving his mother the sole provider for the family. Financially it wasn't the best of circumstances while he grew up. Grant did attend college and graduated with a bachelor's degree in accounting. Aside from graduating college, he still had no real direction and ended up selling drugs. Grant tells a story of how he had gotten robbed and seriously injured. It was the wakeup call he needed and he eventually checked himself into a rehab facility. It was the same one his twin brother had gotten out of recently.

He finished the rehab program and got into selling cars. That's where he started his journey; he soon became one of the hardest working employees within the company and shortly after became a top sales rep. He eventually left the car industry and began a career in sales. Grant Cardone has created multiple companies throughout the years, consisting of Cardone Acquisitions, The Cardone Group, and Cardone Enterprises. He became the CEO of Freedom Motorsports and developed a show on National Geographic called the Turnaround Kings. He is the author of seven books and is a New York Times bestselling author. He is a social media expert with more than $350 million in real estate holdings.

He is the visionary and creator behind 10X and has created a movement behind the brand, helping millions of entrepreneurs all over the world create massive success. I am personally a student of this man and again owe a huge thank you for all the sacrifices and hard work he has put into making other people's lives better. With intense focus and belief, Grant Cardone was able to turn his dreams into reality and today works harder than ever to achieve an even higher goal of becoming a billionaire. Grant Cardone has helped raise millions for charities and is a huge advocate for giving back.

"Show up early, treat people with respect and perform at the highest levels till the world can't deny you." Grant Cardone

Ellen DeGeneres was born in 1958 in Metairie, Louisiana into a loving family along with her older brother. Her parents divorced when she was thirteen years old and Ellen stayed with her mother in Louisiana. She spent her childhood in the inner city, where she loved to ride her bike. Ellen graduated from high school in 1976 and started working at a local law firm. She bounced between jobs during the next few years, never feeling satisfied with her work. When Ellen turned twenty-three she put together a comedy routine for friends and family. She quickly started performing for larger crowds and gaining confidence. The following year she entered a national talent contest put on by the TV network Showtime. She won and earned the title the "Funniest Person in America," being recognized as the country's new up-and-coming comedian.

Over the next few years, Ellen traveled the country performing her stand-up routine. In 1986, she made history as the first comedian to be interviewed by Johnny Carson on *The Tonight Show*. She went on to act in a few movies and TV shows in the '90s. In 1997, she was a guest on the *Oprah Winfrey Show* and came out as a lesbian. In 2003 she became a household name by doing the voiceover for Dory in *Finding Nemo*. In 2016 she was the main voiceover in *Finding Dory*.

Within that span of thirteen years, Ellen had her own talk show, hosted the Academy Awards, the Grammy Awards, and the Primetime Emmys. She was also on one season of *American Idol*. She starred in her own eponymous sitcom and has created a lifestyle brand called ED Ellen DeGeneres. During her illustrious career, Ellen has won twenty People's Choice Awards and thirty Emmys along with countless other awards for her charitable contributions. Ellen's life and career are a prime example of exactly what you can achieve if you never give up and work hard.

Ellen's career is impressive, but I reference her in this book not because of her career in comedy and television but because of her charitable contributions. Ellen has used her status and own money to help millions of people around the world. She gave $1 million to help the victims of Hurricane Harvey, provided full scholarships to seniors at Summit Academy, and has donated $100,000 to stop illegal elephant hunting by banning the importation of elephant hunting trophies. Ellen partnered with Lowe's and donated over half a million dollars to rebuild a rundown school. Ellen also partnered with Dierks Bentley to give an impoverished military family a check for $50,000. Ellen raised over $3.3 million just from a selfie taken at the Oscars. St. Jude's Children's Hospital took half and the other half went to the Humane Society. Ellen DeGeneres is an example of a star achieving goals and helping others.

"We need more kindness, more compassion, more joy, and more laughter. I definitely want to contribute to that." Ellen DeGeneres

6

TIME MANAGEMENT

I believe that time management is a vital tool that can be used to create success within one's life. Bill Gates, Donald Trump, and Michael Jordan have the same twenty-four hours that everyone else has in a day. I believe the difference is that they know how to utilize time very proficiently. The more success I achieved, the better I would need to get with becoming proficient with time management. I remember reading that Bill Gates and Elon Musk both plan their days in five- minute increments.

I understood that the majority of my thoughts pertained to past events. While I believe that I can learn from my past, I also understand that I shouldn't dwell on it either. I wanted to start having the majority of my thoughts pertain to present and future events. When I focused the majority of my thoughts on past events, I allowed the present moment to slip away. I wanted to make a change—I wanted to start living for the future. The same can be said about overthinking future events, like deciding an outcome of an event that hasn't even taken place. I regularly kept myself up at night thinking about everything that could happen within the next few days. Rarely did the event have the outcome that I expected. This kept me from much needed sleep and caused more stress. Over time I worked on always doing my best, treating everyone with respect, and making sound business decisions. I stopped worrying about future outcomes and reacted to present events happening in my life. I understood that I had no control over what hadn't happened yet and how others may treat me at a later date. Just like dwelling on the past, pondering future outcomes took my attention away from what life has to offer me in the present moment.

I read in a few articles that concentration and attention are heightened in the morning, so it would be an optimal time for me to complete important tasks. I started setting aside these hours for growth within my companies.

I found that my focus, memory, and imagination flourished within the early morning hours. Each day I identify three to four tasks that will grow my business. I have focused on creating my mentorship program, writing books, creating clothing lines, making very important calls, and learning. They became my power hours. I have increased my time management skills and felt like I have seen better outcomes within my business and self-growth.

Another tool that I implement when setting goals is the S.M.A.R.T. methodology.

Specific—Being specific about your goals is a vital part to achieving success. Keep clarity within your goals. Simplicity is key and always know your how, your why, and your when. Timeframes are great to keep you on track to reach your particular goal.

Example: Not specific—I want to earn $1 million. Specific—I want to create an online pet clothing store, name it "Hot Dogs," use PPC "Pay-per-click" and SEO "Strategic Engine Optimization" along with Facebook advertising to generate traffic, and have sales totaling $100,000 monthly.

Measurable—You need to be able to measure your progress toward each goal. This will give you the momentum needed to keep moving forward. If you are not reaching your goals you may lose the focus and drive needed to become unstoppable. If you do not measure your progress you can start to feel lost, start to doubt yourself, become overwhelmed, and could become depressed. By measuring your progress, you know exactly where you are in achieving your goals and what steps you still need to take to realize your accomplishments.

Attainable—Setting attainable goals is very important so that you keep a strong mindset. You stay on that high of attaining what you set out to get and you are one more step in the right direction. It is important that you make sure your goals are attainable. Keeping unrealistic goals will place you on the fast track to failure.

Relevant—Make sure the goals you are setting are relevant to what you are trying to attain. This is very simple but oftentimes overlooked. To help yourself stay focused, ask questions such as, why do I want to achieve this goal? What are the objectives to reach this goal?

Timely—Set daily, weekly, and monthly timeframes to help reach your goals. Hold yourself accountable and get a mentor. Make sure to set realistic timeframes for your goals. Focus on being able to achieve those goals so that the positive feelings you get as a result can help you build up momentum.

By utilizing the S.M.A.R.T. methodology I have become more proficient at setting goals, meeting deadlines, and making sure my goals are specific to what I am trying to achieve. This has been an essential part in creating successful businesses.

I had issues with prioritization and what needed to be accomplished for me to achieve the goals I set for myself. I wasn't sure how to set daily priorities; everything felt like it had the same importance level. I broke down my daily tasks and came up with five important tasks that would move my business in a forward direction. I used the early morning hours to make seller and buyer calls, schedule important meetings, answer time sensitive emails, and meditate. I practice each morning to be more charismatic, alert, happy, and focused, which in turn creates a better outcome for my business. I always start my early morning tasks with the mindset of helping people. I do not focus on trying to sell, but more on offering value to my customer. Since I have implemented this strategy I have seen steady growth within my business. I will say that the feeling I get from truly caring about the people I come in contact with fills me with joy.

Each day I take time to identify which tasks are urgent versus important. Urgent tasks include items that need to get done that day, which I then make time for at the end of the work. The import tasks, which are beneficial to the growth of my company but are not as time sensitive, get completed the following morning. Some business professionals advise to complete lengthier tasks first, but sometimes I find it's satisfying to check off several minor tasks first! Staying organized is something that I had to work on as well. The more successful I became, the more organization became important within the business. When

I first created my business I had a few phone calls to make daily, but as my business grew I started to make twenty to thirty important calls a day. Staying organized helped with achieving all of the tasks I set for myself daily.

Having a daily and monthly planner plays a vital role in attaining my goals. I read in many books that successful, goal-oriented people write down their goals every day. Multiple scientific studies have proven that writing down daily tasks and goals maintains your focus, mental fortitude, growth, and a sense of accomplishment. I make sure to write down my goals every morning. I utilize a daily planner in increments of hours. I have an oversized monthly wall calendar on which I write down important events that I don't want to forget. I also complete a weekly report each Sunday that asks questions such as:

How many calls did I make?
How many offers did I make?
What mistakes did I think I made this week?
What were some of the rejections I encountered?
How did I handle those rejections?

How can I do things differently and more productive next week?

By utilizing this weekly report, I grade my performance each week. I highly recommend using these questions in order to correct any inefficiencies within your weekly performance.

Delegation is the transfer of authority by one group or person to another. It was imperative to the growth of my business. When I delegated tasks I improved on my communication skills, built trust, spread innovation, and worked on my leadership skills. I had to learn how to delegate simply because if I wanted to achieve the success I was after I could not go at it alone. I needed to build a team of dedicated professionals, all working to achieve the company's desired goals. I faced much trial and error with hiring people. I quickly understood that being the boss and giving people tasks was not easy. I found out that I had to be 100 percent clear with what I expected out of the new hire. I could not assume or give vague tasking. This led to miscommunication, which in hindsight was my fault. As hard as it was for me, I started taking blame for every outcome within my business, customers, and the people I hired. Once I placed the responsibility on myself for every outcome, I experienced a different thought process, which in turn helped me create the outcome that I wanted. I was able to make the correct decisions to dictate the outcome before it happened in some instances.

Procrastination stopped the forward progression of my business in a huge way. Procrastination is a dream killer—in the beginning I let this infringe on achieving any success. The longer I held off a certain task, the harder it became to start. I later learned that taking action alleviated procrastination. It is my belief that fear is the mind's natural response for self-preservation. I began to use fear as an indicator in which direction I should move. I wanted to be outside of my comfort zone, which is where I would experience the most growth. By constantly using fear as my compass and staying outside my comfort zone I experienced the most growth mentally, physically, and spiritually

TAKING ACTION <u>ALLEVIATES</u> PROCRASTINATION

PROCRASTINATION IS A DREAM KILLER

BECOME AN ACTION TAKER

BECOME UNSTOPPABLE

"My procrastination which has held me back was born of fear…. Now I know that to conquer fear I must always act without hesitation and the flutters in my heart will vanish. Now I know that action reduces the lion of terror…. I will walk where the failure fears to walk." Og Mandino—author and philanthropist whose books have sold over 50 million copies worldwide

7

MONEY MANAGEMENT

I never learned money management in school.

While the core subjects are important, it's nice to see more and more middle schools and high schools introducing life management classes that focus on real-world skills like balancing a check book, investing, and even something as basic as counting money and making change.

I needed a complete overhaul on my perception of money. I was brought up with ideals such as:

More money, more problems.
Money doesn't make you happy.
Money can't buy you happiness.
Money isn't that important.

It is my belief that true happiness comes from helping and giving to others, not financial gains. I understood that if I wanted to achieve the success that I was after, I would need to change my mentality of money.

Without the proper education of money management, I felt like I could misuse the money I earned and could end up losing it all. I grew up hearing stories about lottery winners regretting their windfalls because they came into large amounts of money without the proper management skills and squandered their great fortunes. With great amounts of money comes great responsibility. Those who don't know how to manage money, no matter the amount, may risk losing it.

Two examples that I want to reference are Mike Tyson and Evander Holyfield, two of the world's greatest heavyweight boxers. Both were worth more than $100 million in their prime and both ended up filing for bankruptcy. I believe that the road to riches is best driven slowly so that you can make your mistakes with smaller amounts of money along the way. Working over several years to amass a fortune may help you appreciate the value of money you have worked so hard to earn. I understand that I need to enjoy the ride, not just the destination. I realized I first needed to control myself in order to have control over the money I obtained.

Since I had never had any classes on money management, I started out by learning the fundamentals.

Money management tips I started implementing:
1. I kept track of the money I spent in a checkbook.
2. I tried living within my means.
3. I bought more of what I needed and less of what I wanted.
4. I set up a savings account, placing 10 percent of earned income in the account
5. I decided what my money was going to be spent on before I spent it.
6. I started giving a percentage of my money each Sunday at church.
7. I started using cash to make purchases.
8. I decreased how much I impulse buy.

9. I became money conscious.

These are a few quick tips that helped me get on the right track. The most important money management tip that I started implementing was simply becoming money conscious. I started to live within my means and stopped impulse buying to a large degree. A few simple techniques that helped me become debt-free within one year are listed below:

I started to implement the five-second rule. Anytime I was about to spend money I took five seconds and asked myself "am I about to purchase a want or a need?" If the purchase fell into the latter category, then I asked myself if I could potentially purchase the item for less. If the item fell in the want category I would simply put back the item more often than not. Thinking before making purchases helped me to prevent impulse buying, which in turn made me more aware of my financial spending habits. With companies spending millions on Facebook, YouTube, TV, radio, and billboard advertising combined with the ease and quickness of a credit card swipe, it was no wonder why I had terrible spending habits. I became conscious of the bombardment of advertisements and started to implement the five second rule, which worked very well for taking me out of the consumer cycle.

A few real-world examples of how I use the five-second rule in my daily life include:

At the grocery store right before check out, I look in my cart and decide what I really need as opposed to what I want. The chocolate-covered coffee beans and the bottle of wine go back on the shelf (of course one bottle of wine is left in the cart) and I've just saved myself $20! So easy, yet so effective. When I'm clothes shopping, I put back two or three of my least favorite items and that usually saves me $50 to $100. While implementing this rule at restaurants, I was pleasantly surprised to find that the specials are usually cheaper than the regular items on the menu. As an added bonus, the specials are often healthy alternatives to my old favorites. It's a win-win! This simple but effective strategy can alter your financial situation for the better. Implement this into your daily life and you could pay off a $5,000 credit card balance in five months just by saving $250 a week.

Albert Einstein was quoted saying, "Compound interest is the eighth wonder of the world. He who understands it, earns it. He who doesn't, pays it." Wise investments can have substantial life-changing returns. By placing $2,000 in an eighteen-year-old's investment account for eight years he would become a multi-millionaire. At the age of sixty-five, he would have accumulated over $2 million by utilizing the power of compound interest. The initial $16,000 investment would have grown into millions. Compound interest, if utilized correctly, can be the best investment you ever make. The key is to start investing at a young age and allow the compound interest to build over time. You would need to gain knowledge and pick investment funds that could net you 10 to 12 percent interest rate a year. Below is a chart that shows a $16,000 investment turning into a multimillion dollar pay out:

COMPOUND INTEREST

AGE	Brett's Investment	Annual Increase	April's Investment	Annual Increase
18	2,000	2,240	0	0
19	2,000	4,749	0	0
20	2,000	7,542	0	0
21	2,000	10,706	0	0
22	2,000	14,230	0	0
23	2,000	18,175	0	0
24	2,000	22,599	0	0
25	2,000	27,551	0	0
26	0	30,853	2,000	2,240
27	0	34,560	2,000	4,749
28	0	38,708	2,000	7,542
29	0	43,352	2,000	10,706
30	0	48,556	2,000	14,230
31	0	60,910	2,000	18,175
32	0	68,215	2,000	22,599
33	0	76,820	2,000	27,551
34	0	85,490	2,000	30,853
35	0	95,421	2,000	34,560
45	0	238,210	2,000	142,156
55	0	735,982	2,000	481,367
65	0	2,321,852	2,000	1,546,320

Brett started investing at the age of eighteen, $2,000 a year until the age of twenty-five. By utilizing time and interest, his $16,000 dollar investment grew into over a $2 million payout for him at the age of sixty-five. April started investing at the age of twenty-six, $2,000 a year until the age of sixty-five. April invested $79,000 dollars over the span of thirty-nine years. Her $78,000 dollar investment grew into a $1.5 million payout at the age of sixty-five. It is never too late to start investing and utilizing compound interest. Both scenarios could make you a millionaire.

The third technique comes straight from millionaires themselves. It involves how some of the wealthiest people in this country view and spend money. I believe that smart people learn from their mistakes, but smarter people learn from the mistakes of others.

Make your money go to work for you. Start a business, create a blog, create a YouTube channel, invest in other companies, brand yourself, or write a book. These ideas take a relentless mindset, hard work, focus, and perseverance, so find something that you're passionate about and go after it.

Be cautious of lending money. Many of us have our own stories of lending friends and family members money and never getting it back. I like to use the rule that if I get burned once, shame on you. If I get burned twice, shame on me.

Understand what drives you to spend money. Is it fear, happiness, anxiety, or boredom? Figure out which of these is your crutch and replace that action with something else. Example: When I was bored I tended to search Amazon and make many impulse buys. Now I read or watch TV.

Teach your kids about money. I teach my son the value of the dollar by having him complete tasks for money. He then spends money he has earned on items he wants.

Live frugally. It doesn't matter how much money you have if you spend it all. Living frugally comes back to deciding what you need versus what you want. You might want fifty pairs of shoes and three cars, but you probably don't need them.

Create multiple streams of income. In today's marketplace there are many options for creating multiple streams of income. You could create YouTube channels, blogs, and brands or use network marketing, affiliate marketing, investments, and learn about the foreign currency markets. I never want to rely on one business to make up the majority of my income. If there was to be a market crash in real estate I would have my clothing line, foreign currency trading, and speaking engagements to rely on.

Residual monthly income. Earning profits on sales or services that you have generated in the past to produce future revenue is the concept of residual income. I accomplish this by selling products or services that have a monthly, quarterly, semiannual, or annual revolving fee. Usually I profit from a percentage of that fee. The more sales I make, the more my residual monthly income grows.

UNDERSTANDING ASSETS VERSUS LIABILITIES

I believe that the number one reason why so many people are struggling financially is because of their misunderstanding of assets versus liabilities. The equation is simple. Creating assets creates wealth. Having more liabilities than assets can create an unstable financial situation. An asset is something that you own that can provide you with future financial benefit. Cash, land, inventory, and accounts receivable are assets. A liability is an expense. These are considered obligations that you must fulfill that usually consist of money or services. I avoid having more liabilities than assets. I understand that acquiring wealth and obtaining success relies on having numerous amounts of assets.

WEALTH is having an ABUNDANCE of <u>ASSETS.</u>

AVERAGE is having an ABUNDANCE of <u>LIABILITIES</u>.

Homes that don't produce income are liabilities. My car is a liability. When I travel for pleasure it is a liability and anything that is paid out is considered a liability.

Anything that creates revenue is an asset. When I first started learning about assets and liabilities I inventoried each of mine. This was a great indicator of what I needed to work on. I came up with solutions to minimize my liabilities while increasing my assets.

Adopting these money management practices set me on the right path to creating a better financial future for my family and me. I also took Dave Ramsey's "Financial Peace University" course. I admire Dave Ramsey because he had made and lost a fortune, yet made it again.

"Financial peace isn't the acquisition of stuff. It's learning to live on less than you make, so you can give money back and have money to invest. You can't win until you do this." Dave Ramsey—American businessman, five-time New York Times bestseller and radio host

TAKING ACTION

I understood that taking action was a very important step in obtaining the levels of success I hoped to achieve. If I wanted to become unstoppable I would have to become a relentless action taker, but fear frequently halted my forward momentum. I needed to correct this issue.

Taking massive action needed to become second nature to me. It was something that I needed to work on over time and on a daily basis. I found out that the more action I took the easier it was for me to take the action needed for me to achieve my goals. I didn't realize it at the time, but just like anything, taking action took practice. The more action I took the better I became. Traits of highly successful people consist of taking massive action on a regular basis. I focused my thoughts on only positive outcomes from my actions and that helped alleviate some of the fear I felt while outside my comfort zone.

I knew that I would experience many failures along the way. I had been told by a mentor that I needed to start viewing failure as success. He mentioned success would not exist without failure and vice versa. He recommended that I recondition my thought process to see that failure is a necessary part of achieving success. To this day I view failure as a stepping stone for me to achieve the life that I aspire to have.

For me, taking the first step in any new endeavor tended to be the hardest. Once I took the plunge and started taking action I realized momentum would grow through the achievements that I would obtain. Each little success toward the desired goal grew into something larger over time. In the beginning it was motivation that I lacked, which in time ended up being one of my strong suits. I realized I just needed to take the first step and then I would gain motivation along the way. In the past I tried to gain motivation before I took the action needed for a desired outcome. Once I changed and started taking action, the motivation then followed. I always like to read books on a topic that I'm wanting to learn about. One book that helped me, *The 5 Second Rule* by Mel Robbins, changed the way I took action. She provides a simple tool that is easy to use—it can give you the push needed in order to achieve the life that you desire. I use this tool and saw a massive change within my life. If I knew I needed to do something that was undesirable at the time, I would count back from five seconds. I would then take the action that I was previously not going to take. For example: writing this book. There were countless times I thought about going into my office and continuing to write this book. Every time my mind would come up with something that was more enjoyable to do. I would end up going to the gym or sitting down and watching an episode of my favorite TV show at the time. I would call some friends up and schedule lunch or dinner or come up with an excuse as to why I deserved a day off. Once I started to implement the five second rule, the thought of going into my office and continuing to write my book would resonate. I then would count back from five seconds and take the action I needed in order for me to achieve the goal of finishing my book. I implemented the five second rule into more aspects of my daily routine. This caused me to see more success within my life.

"If you don't start doing the things you don't feel like doing, you will wake up one year from today and be in exactly the same place." Mel Robbins

The more that I avoided instant gratification, the more success I started seeing within my business. I started watching less television, started drinking less, and focused more time and energy on achieving my goals. I eliminated sources of distraction. The larger and more ambitious the goal, the more self-discipline I needed to acquire the desired outcome. *The 10X Rule* inspired me to start taking massive action. Once I read that book, I realized that the key to success in any endeavor was to take massive action. I knew I wanted to achieve a certain type of lifestyle but never understood what it would take. I have read this particular book multiple times. I use it as a tool to inspire me to keep taking high levels of action. Every few months I slow down—I still have the same goals, I just stop taking as much action and find comfort within my successes. I know at that moment, I need to re-read *The 10X Rule* to gain inspiration and continue to keep taking massive amounts of action.

Another tool I use when taking massive action is the process of elimination. When I start any new endeavor I like to try many different methods to achieve a desired outcome. Through split testing and recording the results I am able to see what has the greatest return on investment. I then spend more time, money, and energy in that area of my business. This has led to me seeing more success within my business and an increase in profits. Through using the process of elimination I learned to work smarter, not harder. I was always under the impression that the harder you work, the more success you will inevitably have. I do believe that you must work hard, but taking the correct actions are also just as important to achieving the success you desire. Once I started replicating myself within the business with new hires, I was able to focus more on increasing revenue and had more freedom. I believe that a business with one sole employee has a frail infrastructure. There is a saying in business, "The most dangerous number in business to have is the number one." One of anything is not a good number to have, including one employee, one customer, one supplier, or one lead source. If my one hire quits, or the one supplier I had went out of business, my business would take a drastic hit. For this reason, I make sure to employ multiple people and always have multiple contacts within the business that can provide me with the same level of expertise. I often call lead generating companies and review them based on price, quality and quantity of leads, and past reviews from customers.

Taking action is an essential piece to the puzzle. I was looking for longevity, so I took time in the beginning to build a solid foundation. I knew that troubles were an inevitable part of creating new successes. I made sure I planned ahead so if something bad were to happen I would not be left standing with one of anything. I became knowledgeable on many different ways to create leads for my company. I hired two assistants, two real estate agents, had multiple contracting crews, and knew many closing attorneys around the area. If relationships went south or companies moved or went out of business, I could make quick and easy replacements where need be. I also purchased services that would protect my personal and business name in case of any litigious activity. This is the solid foundation on which I built my company.

When I first started taking massive action I tended to have great weeks and then the following weeks I was completely distracted or unmotivated. One strategy I implemented was to have other people hold me accountable. I was in a mentorship program at the time. I highly recommend that you get into one as well. I had an accountability call each week with my coach. Each week the call would consist of what was going on within my business and whether I achieved the goals I told her during our last conversation. If I didn't achieve my goals, we would discuss why. After, I would set new goals for the upcoming week and that process continued throughout the year. If you don't have the means to hire an accountability coach, I would suggest telling a close friend or relative that is interested in what you're trying to accomplish. Tell them what you plan to do in conversation. Just telling other people what your goals are can have a profound impact if you are successful in completing the goals you set for yourself.

In the earlier years of my life, I lived by the mantra "when the time is right." This meant I would hold off plans and dreams because I always told myself when the time is right I would take the first step. Years passed and the right time never presented itself. I stopped waiting for the perfect conditions and became an action taker. I started taking action on a daily basis. Only then did I see my dreams start to take shape. I spent countless years thinking about my dreams and successes that I wanted to achieve, but never once taking the necessary action to see them through. I used excuses to justify my current situation. Now, I take responsibility for every occurrence within my life. I understand that life happens because of me and not to me. Hindsight is 20/20; if I could sit down and have a conversation with the younger me, I would say stop making excuses, start taking action, and go after your dreams. The only one that is holding you back is yourself. Oh yeah, and stop caring what other people think of you. The world deserves to meet the person you are meant to become.

Staying positive and enthusiastic in my beliefs is a shortcut to success. Everyone that I come in contact with I try my best to be positive and enthusiastic around. I found out that opportunities present themselves much more when I present these traits. People are drawn to others with such energies. I realized that if I was negative around a positive person we ended up not speaking. On the other hand, if I walk in that same room with a smile on my face, make eye contact, and say a few very positive things about his outfit, we become best friends. I use compliments to start a conversation quite a bit. It usually leads to a fruitful relationship.

Once I started working on bettering my communication skills the world around me started taking shape. I used to think that it was everyone else that dictated how my life had turned out. I remember blaming other people and circumstances for what I had in life. Now, I understand that I can create my own reality to a certain extent. There are always external forces at play, but the majority of circumstances I can control. Every day I work on bettering my understanding of how certain people perceive a particular situation. In doing this, I can communicate from a place of understanding and compassion. When I approach a conversation with this in mind I tend to have more control of a favorable outcome.

I quickly saw success and became complacent within my actions. My business maintained profit margins but strained to see new growth. In order to achieve my dreams I knew that I must do things that I had never done before. I used this as a reference point for growth within my company. If I never talked to a private money lender before about acquired $1 million, I knew in order to see growth that would need to be the next step. The actions that I was taking at the time created a six-figure income, but to achieve a $1 million annual profit I would have to do things within my business that I hadn't done before.

I would tell my younger self not to become complacent: communication and compassion are key, dream big, stay positive and enthusiastic, treat everyone the way you would want to be treated, enjoy the ride, take massive consistent action, and never give up.

"The ability to discipline yourself to delay gratification in the short term in order to enjoy greater rewards in the long term, is the indispensable prerequisite for success." Brian Tracy—public speaker, self-development teacher, author to over seventy books, and CEO to three successful companies

9

UNSTOPPABLE

This chapter illustrates what my life looks like today and how I achieved a six-figure income while working full-time in the United States Coast Guard. Since I changed my thought process, whom I surround myself with, and my daily actions, I am able to leave active duty status with the United States Coast Guard next summer and focus on real estate investing full time. Within one year, I successfully self-published this book, created a six-figure earning real estate investing company, the clothing line Unstoppable, and the mentorship program Motivation to Millions, became debt free, and learned Forex, foreign currency trading, along with raising over $400,000 in private funding that I used to buy properties and fix them up to make large profits.

According to the Merriam Webster dictionary, the definition of unstoppable is "incapable of being stopped." I decided to become a creator and turn my visions into reality, incapable of being stopped. Along with some guidance from my mother, this is how the title of this book came to be. Not only is this book dedicated to her, but she also played a pivotal role in coming up with its title.

I made sure to leave the universe no other choice but to provide what I am asking for. I faced countless rejections and failures along the way and still have a long way to go, but deep down I know that I will see my visions take shape and my dreams become reality. There is no other path, for I am a creator and unstoppable. I want you to overcome every obstacle you will face in reaching your goals and in doing so you will become unstoppable, too.

In chapter two you found out what my life looked like when I held down an unsatisfying full-time job and was content with my status in life. My days were filled with little ambition, not much focus, and no faith in myself. I surrounded myself with good people, but they had low drive and ambition. At thirty years old, the last book I read was *To Kill a Mockingbird*, and that was in eighth grade. I drank a bit too much and didn't set any goals for myself outside of the next weekend. I never thought about what my life could be like if I stepped outside of my comfort zone and chased my dreams. To be completely honest, at that time, I didn't even know that being uncomfortable could be a good thing. I didn't like failure so I stayed with what I knew. Doing so kept me in the exact same spot year after year.

As I started reading books and expanding my mind, my journey began. Within that moment my life was changed forever. Now with a successful company, sixty books or so that I have read, and a date to get out of the Coast Guard, I will lay out what an average week looks like for me.

I wake up each morning at an early hour. A few days a week I focus on ten minutes of meditation. Other days I focus on self-affirmations. I use this free time in the mornings to work on my most important tasks.

I started taking my diet a lot more seriously, adding whole grains, eggs, and a nutritional shake to my breakfast each morning. I find that I don't have any sugar crashes throughout the day and my clarity and focus are heightened.

I still leave the house in my convertible Camaro, but with the second house I renovated I was able to pay the car off completely. Instead of blaring the radio to a hot new song, I switch it up a few days a week and spend the fifteen-minute car ride into work listening to a new book. If I'm really interested in the book, some weeks I will listen to the book every morning. I still like to jam out on my way to work, especially on Fridays.

Once at work I spend my time getting my work done—during my lunch break I make necessary phone calls. I started bringing my lunch to work. When I cut soda and fast food out of my diet, I immediately felt so much better. I still love to eat out and do so on the weekends but make sure to stick to a pretty clean diet throughout the week. I also started drinking a lot more water.

I added a regular workout routine into my daily regimen. I started taking essential daily vitamins to increase my memory, mental focus, and overall health. A game changer for me is that I started listening to my books while working out. I believe moderation is key for longevity, so I listen to my books a few days a week and the other days I play my favorite music, which allows me to zone out and be completely in the moment.

When I get home from the gym I take a shower and go straight to my office. Every day I focus on growing my business. I make sure to be working on my business and not in my business. This is a vital factor in me achieving success within my company. Too many times I found myself working in my business, which consisted of cleaning out my inbox, responding to Facebook posts, making business cards, creating road signs, building websites, or organizing my office.

Now I spend those two hours prospecting buyers, speaking with home sellers, and speaking to new potential private money lenders. I center my focus on bringing in new revenue for my company. I believe that too many new businesses focus on working on their company's "busy work" and not focusing on generating new revenue, which is the life blood. After a few hours in my office I relax and cook dinner, then watch an episode of my favorite series on Netflix. A few days a week I take my longboard out and cruise down the boardwalk or go on a nice walk and enjoy the sunset overlooking the ocean.

I get home about 9 p.m. and learn a new system that generates leads or listen to an episode of the latest Bigger Pockets podcast, a real estate investing tool. Then I go to sleep around 10:30 p.m. This is my weekly routine from Monday through Friday. Some of the biggest changes I made from my average lifestyle consisted of time management, reading, and learning on a daily basis. I focus more on my health, wealth, success, and happiness.

I would not have seen the success that I saw in one year if it wasn't for me changing my circle of influence and gaining the right mentors. In doing so I listened, learned, and implemented the lessons taught to me by people who have reached the success I hope to obtain. On the weekends I drive to my properties and complete any necessary work. I schedule appointments for buyers and sellers during the weekends, although I can occasionally see clients during the week after work hours. I didn't have to become an overworked robot and hate my life in order to achieve success. The more time I spend chasing my dreams, the sooner they become my reality. If I overwork myself, I can become unmotivated and uninterested in trying to achieve the life I truly desire.

I chose the work smarter, not harder approach. I started reading self-help books, business books, and reached out to successful people. I strive to adhere to my regimented way of life, but of course there are times when I sleep late, eat fast food, and chill out on the couch at night instead of making cold calls to bring in new business. When I do slip like this, I don't punish myself. Instead, I wake up the next morning and continue on my road to becoming unstoppable!

Surround yourself with amazing people, strive for greatness, always be a student, dream big, and make things happen.

"Draw your line in the sand. Make your decision now and start taking action to really live your dream. By not taking bold steps to live your dream, not only are you missing out on fully living, but the world is missing out on the greatness you have to offer. Be bold!" Les Brown

10

FRUITION

I hope you use this information to achieve your

own successes and increase your overall happiness in life.
If this book inspires just one individual to reach their
dreams, the time and effort I put into it will be worth it.
The more successful I become, the more I give back to my
community and charitable organizations. This book is part
of me paying it forward.

I laid out the skills I acquired for me to envision and
manifest the thoughts in my mind. In creating my own
reality I started thriving, not just surviving. The feelings
that surround living life on my own terms should be
experienced by anyone who wishes for them. This is why I
laid out a road map to El Dorado, the city of gold. With
patience, persistence, and the right direction, anything is

possible. I have provided the direction—now it's up to you to take the first step.

"You will never fail until you stop trying." Albert Einstein

After reading some of the bestselling self-help and entrepreneurial books, I have noticed a similarity. The majority of the books have been written well into the author's successful career. Since I have much success to achieve, I wanted to take this time and make a few predictions about my own life. I'm a firm believer that life happens because of you and not to you. I will use the methods in the previous chapters to continue to create the life of my dreams.

Thoughts that are going to take shape:

1. Have a book on the New York Times best-sellers list.
2. Become the owner of a multi-million dollar real estate investing company, Saxman Realty LLC.

3. Be a guest on the *Ellen DeGeneres Show*.

4. Write at least two more books.

5. Buy my mother her dream house.

6. Become a professional speaker.

7. Donate $50,000 to the Make-A-Wish Foundation.

This book is filled with inspirational quotes from some of the most successful and imaginative people throughout history. I have compiled all my knowledge on becoming truly unstoppable in any endeavor with the hopes that you will take the necessary actions to change the world around you for the better, all the while creating the life of your dreams.

Jesus said, "If you have faith as small as a mustard seed, you can say to this mountain; move from here to there, and it will move. Nothing will be impossible for you." Go out and do great things, my friends.

Sincerely,

Joseph R. Saxman

To get the full list of books that have helped change my life or to learn more about my mentorship program Motivation to Millions,
 go to
www.be-unstoppable.com

RECOMMENDED READING

1. *The Divine Matrix* by Gregg Braden
2. *The Greatest Salesman in the World* by Og Mandino
3. *The Richest Man in Babylon* by George S. Clason
4. *The 10X Rule* by Grant Cardone
5. *Multiple Streams of Income* by Gregg Braden
6. *Think and Grow Rich* by Napoleon Hill
7. *Go for No!: Yes is the Destination* by Richard Fenton & Andrea Waltz
8. *The Four Agreements* by Don Miguel Ruiz
9. *The Power of Consistency* by Weldon Long
10. *The Magic of Believing* by Claude M. Bristol. I saved the best for last, the book that I have credited with changing my life.

AUTHOR'S NOTE

Four pieces of information that I would like for you to retain from reading this book are as follows:

1. The unstoppable formula:

   o TAKING ACTION <u>ALLEVIATES</u> PROCRASTINATION
   o PROCRASTINATION IS A DREAM KILLER
   o BECOME AN ACTION TAKER
   o BECOME UNSTOPPABLE

2. Failure is success.

3. Live outside your comfort zone.

4. Be compassionate.

If you would like to learn more from me, I am more than happy to teach you. I have paid more than $50,000 in mentorship programs within the last few years. I continue to expand my knowledge in the self-help realm as well as in real estate investing. I believe that they go hand-in-hand. Although my mentorship programs have been highly effective, it was a very high price to enter the real estate investing market. I created a mentorship program with the most current and cost-effective methods to finding, funding, and flipping properties around the country. Finding funding is a major hurdle people face when getting into this market. A high percentage of companies that offer funding for investment properties require past HUD statements from previous flips you've completed. This is why I raised enough private funding for each and every one of my students. My mentorship program offers 100 percent funding for investment opportunities across the country. This program gives you an inside look into the methods that my company currently uses to procure deals within the marketplace. You can make $20,000 to $80,000 in profit per deal using my methods. I know you can because I do!

To learn more go to:

WWW.BE-UNSTOPPABLE.COM

Made in the USA
Columbia, SC
10 March 2019